A gift from your Mother

From Mother, With Love ♡ ♡ ♡

A FILL-IN-THE-BLANK KEEPSAKE
OF MOM'S LIFE

BY ALEX A. LLUCH

WS Publishing Group
San Diego, California

A GIFT FROM YOUR MOTHER

By Alex A. Lluch
Published by WS Publishing Group
San Diego, California 92119
© Copyright 2009 by WS Publishing Group

Design by:
Sarah Jang, WS Publishing Group
Interior Graphic/Frames: ©iStockphoto.com/friztin

For more information on this and many other best-selling books visit:
www.WSPublishingGroup.com.
E-mail: info@WSPublishingGroup.com

ISBN 13: 978-1-934386-61-3

Printed in China

CONTENTS

ALL ABOUT MOTHER

Your full name: ....

Birthday: ....

Hometown: ....

Your current age: ....

How old do you feel inside? ....

Your favorite age to be, and why? ....

Your motto: ....

....

....

....

....

Your heroes: ....

....

Three words that best describe you: ....

....

....

"God could not be everywhere and therefore he made mothers."
~ Jewish Proverb

Place a favorite
picture of you
here.

A Favorite Photo

....

....

★ FAMILY TREE

A memory of your father from childhood: ....
....
....

A memory of your mother: ....
....
....

Do you better resemble your father or mother? ....

What personality traits did you get from your mother? ....
....

Which did you get from your father? ....
....

A fond memory of your siblings: ....
....
....

Who in your family are you closest to? ....
....

"Families are like fudge — mostly sweet with a few nuts."
~ Anonymous ★

FAMILY TREE

....
Grandfather

| Your
| Family

....
Grandfather

....
Grandmother

....
Grandmother

....
Mother

....
Father

....
Sibling

....
Sibling

....
Sibling

....
You

....
Sibling

Family pets: ....

....

Other significant family members: ....

....

....

....

★ FAMILY TREE

Did you have a favorite aunt or uncle? ....

....

Favorite cousin? ....

What was your favorite holiday? ....

Did you take any memorable vacations as a family? ....

....

....

Who was your most influential family member? ....

....

Are there any family members you wish I could have met before they passed away? ....

....

Are there any special recipes that have been passed down through your family? ....

....

....

....

....

"The love of a family is life's greatest blessing."
~ Anonymous ★

Place
memorabilia
relating to your
family here.

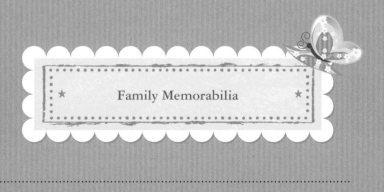

★ Family Memorabilia ★

★ FAMILY TREE

Where were your ancestors from? ....

....

Any famous relatives in your lineage? ....

....

Did your family practice any cultural or ethnic traditions? ....

....

Was there ever a time your entire family got together? What was the occasion? ....

....

A family event that really impacted you: ....

....

....

One thing you are grateful your parents taught you: ....

....

....

One person in your family you wish you were closer to: ....

....

"A happy family is but an earlier heaven."
~ George Bernard Shaw ★

Place a photo
of ancestors or
distant relatives
here.

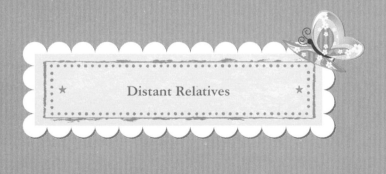

Distant Relatives

★ GRANDPARENTS

What were your maternal grandparents like? ....

....

Where did they live? ....

Describe a favorite memory of spending time with them: ....

....

What were your paternal grandparents like? ....

....

Where did they live? ....

What is a special memory of them? ....

....

Did they tell you stories about your father as a boy? ....

....

....

Have you heard stories about your mother? ....

....

....

"Grandmas are moms with lots of frosting."
~ Anonymous ★

Place photos of one or both sets of grandparents here.

Grandparents

....

....

★ PARENTS

How did your parents meet? ....

....

What was the date of their wedding? ....

Did they stay married? ....

What did your parents do for a living? ....

....

Did you have any family traditions? ....

....

....

Did your mother make you any special meals as a child? ....

....

What was your favorite thing to do with your mom? ....

....

Your favorite thing to do with your dad? ....

....

....

"You don't choose your family. They are God's gift to you,
as you are to them." ~ Desmond Tutu ★

Place a photo
of your parents
here.

Parents

★ PARENTS

What did you admire about your parents? ....

....

What did they hope you would become? ....

Did they ever embarrass you? ....

....

What qualities did they want to pass down to you? ....

....

How are you similar to your mother? ....

....

How are you very different? ....

How are you similar to your father? ....

....

How are you very different? ....

Who did you get along with better, and why? ....

....

....

"We never know the love of our parents for us
till we have become parents." ~ Henry Ward Beecher ★

PARENTS

What is the best advice your parents ever gave you? ....

....

....

....

....

....

....

....

....

....

....

....

....

....

★ SIBLINGS

You were the: oldest   /   youngest   /   middle child

What did you like about your birth order? ....

....

What did you dislike? ....

....

Was there a sibling you were particularly close to? ....

....

Your favorite game to play with siblings: ....

What did you make-believe together? ....

What did you fight with your siblings over? ....

....

A time you got in big trouble: ....

....

Describe the nicest thing a sibling ever did for you: ....

....

....

"Brothers and sisters are as close as hands and feet."
~ Vietnamese Proverb ★

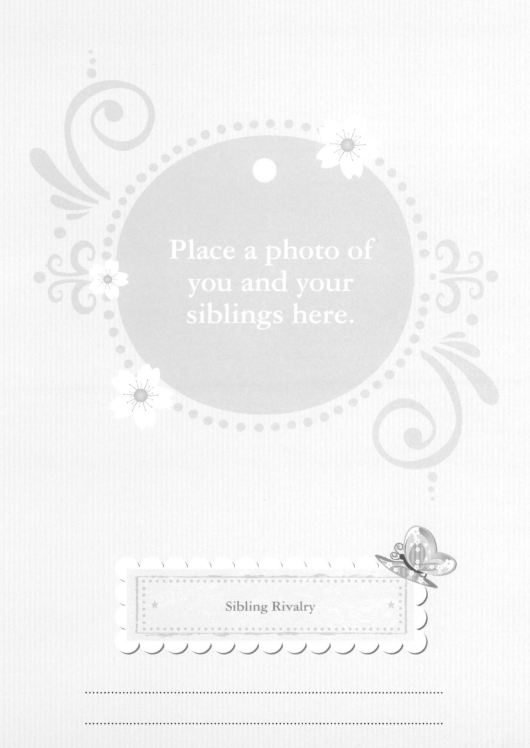

Place a photo of you and your siblings here.

Sibling Rivalry

....

....

★ GROWING UP

Where you grew up: ....

What was your hometown like? ....

....

What did you like best about growing up there? ....

....

Do you know what your first word was? ....

What kind of baby were you? ....

Your very first memory: ....

....

Your first address: ....

Childhood nicknames: ....

Describe your childhood in one sentence: ....

....

Most valuable lesson as a child: ....

....

....

"That's the real trouble with the world,
too many people grow up." ~ Walt Disney ★

Place a favorite photo of you as a child here.

Childhood Fun

....

....

GROWING UP

Your very first friend: ....

How did you meet? ....

....

....

What were your childhood pets? ....

....

How did you choose your pets' names? ....

A favorite memory of your pets: ....

....

....

Did you have an imaginary friend as a child? ....

Did you have a treehouse, fort, or secret hideout? ....

Favorite thing to do in the summer: ....

....

Favorite thing to do in the winter: ....

....

"The most effective kind of education is that
a child should play amongst lovely things." ~ Plato

GROWING UP

Who were your childhood best friends? Describe a favorite memory of spending time with your

childhood friends. Do you still keep in touch with any childhood friends? ....

....

....

....

....

....

....

....

....

....

....

....

....

....

GROWING UP

What were your favorite childhood hobbies or pastimes? ....

....

....

Your favorite book as a child: ....

Favorite food: ....

Favorite board game: ....

Favorite TV show: ....

Favorite song: ....

Favorite outfit: ....

Favorite flavor of ice cream: ....

Favorite place to play: ....

Did you collect anything? ....

....

....

Do you still have that collection? ....

....

"Anyone who keeps the ability to see beauty never grows old."
~ Franz Kafka

GROWING UP

What are some smells, tastes, and sounds that remind you of your childhood? Describe what each represents to you. ....

....

....

....

....

....

....

....

....

....

....

....

....

....

....

★ GROWING UP

Do you recall the price of things when you were growing up?

Movie ticket: ....

Gallon of gas: ....

Soda: ....

Milk: ....

Postage stamp: ....

Ice cream cone: ....

Car: ....

College tuition: ....

Minimum wage: ....

Other: ....

Did you get an allowance as a child? How much was it? ....

What did you buy? ....

....

What was one thing you wanted but couldn't afford? ....

....

*"I am not afraid of tomorrow, for I have seen yesterday
and I love today." ~ William Allen White* ★

GROWING UP

Write about a significant world event that occurred when you were growing up. ....

....

....

....

....

....

....

....

....

....

....

....

....

....

★ EDUCATION

What was the name of your first school? ....

Who was your favorite teacher, and why? ....

....

What kind of student were you? ....

....

Did you ever get sent to the principal's office? ....

....

....

Which subjects did you enjoy in school? ....

Which subjects did you dread? ....

Did you play sports while you were in school? ....

Any instruments? ....

Were you in any clubs? ....

Did you have an after-school job? ....

....

....

"You must learn day by day, year by year,
to broaden your horizon." ~ Ethel Barrymore ★

EDUCATION

Describe your proudest moment in school. Perhaps you were graduating or winning an award or trophy. ....

....

....

....

....

....

....

....

....

....

....

....

....

....

....

★ EDUCATION

Were you popular in school? ....

How would other students describe you? A nerd, jock, wallflower, etc? ....

....

Did you have a boyfriend in school? What was he like? ....

....

Did you ever attend Prom? If so, who was your date? ....

....

What did you wear? ....

....

You were or should have been voted "Most Likely to…" ....

What was your dream for the future post-high school? ....

....

....

If you went to college, what did you study? ....

   Did you ever study in another country? ....

....

"I never let schooling interfere with my education."
~ Mark Twain

Place a photo
of you in school
here.

School Days

....

....

★ A YOUNG ADULT

What was the first job you had? ....

....

How much money did you make? ....

Who taught you how to drive a car? ....

What kind of car did you learn on? ....

What was your first car? How much did it cost? ....

When did you decide on your political affiliation? ....

....

Do you remember who the first president you voted for was? ....

....

Where were you when President John F. Kennedy was shot? ....

....

Did you consider yourself religious as a young adult? ....

....

Did you go to church? ....

....

"Well-behaved women rarely make history."
~ Laurel Thatcher Ulrich ★

A YOUNG ADULT

Describe a personal event that was life-changing for you. What event made you feel like a real adult? ....

....

....

....

....

....

....

....

....

....

....

....

....

....

....

★ WORK LIFE

The first "real" job you had: ....

Worst job: ....

The most exciting or interesting work you ever did: ....

....

Would you rather make a lot of money in a job you hate or make a little money in a job you love?

....

If money were no object, you would have worked as: ....

....

What is your biggest career accomplishment? ....

....

How did you decide whether or not to be a stay-at-home mom? ....

....

The best boss you had: ....

The worst boss: ....

If you won the Lottery, would you continue to work at all? ....

....

"The secret of joy in work is contained in one word — excellence.
To know how to do something well is to enjoy it." ~ Pearl S. Buck ★

WORK LIFE

What would your dream job have been? Describe it in detail here. ....

....

....

....

....

....

....

....

....

....

....

....

....

....

....

....

MAJOR MILESTONES

First time riding a bike: ....

First school dance: ....

First broken bone: ....

First trip to an amusement park: ....

First time you moved out on your own: ....

First roommate: ....

First apartment: ....

Person close to you who got married: ....

Person close to you who died: ....

First time on an airplane: ....

First time you traveled out of the country: ....

A time you were in the newspaper: ....

First time using a computer: ....

Major religious experience: ....

A brush with death: ....

An epiphany you had: ....

"I know who I was when I got up this morning, but I think I
must have been changed several times since then." ~ *Alice in Wonderland*

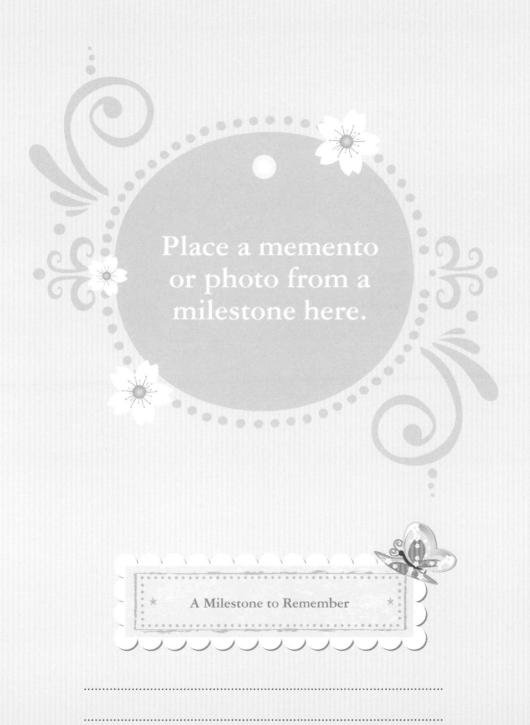

Place a memento or photo from a milestone here.

★ A Milestone to Remember ★

TRIPS & TRAVELS

Your favorite city to visit, and why? ....

....

The most interesting city or country you have visited, and why? ....

....

The most beautiful city or country you have visited: ....

....

The most exotic city or country you have visited: ....

....

Number of states you have lived in: ....

Did you ever want to live in another country? Where? ....

Somewhere you would not be interested in going: ....

Favorite landmark you have visited: ....

Favorite beach vacation: ....

....

Favorite winter vacation: ....

....

"Though we travel the world over to find the beautiful, we must
carry it with us or we find it not." ~ Ralph Waldo Emerson ★

Place a photo from your favorite vacation here.

Favorite Vacation

★ TRIPS & TRAVELS

Your most relaxing vacation: ....

....

Vacation from hell: ....

....

A spontaneous vacation you took: ....

....

An exciting vacation with friends: ....

....

Your most romantic vacation: ....

....

Something you learned about yourself from traveling: ....

....

A time when the weather was perfect: ....

....

A time when the weather was awful: ....

....

.

"One's destination is never a place,
but a new way of seeing things." ~ Henry Miller ★

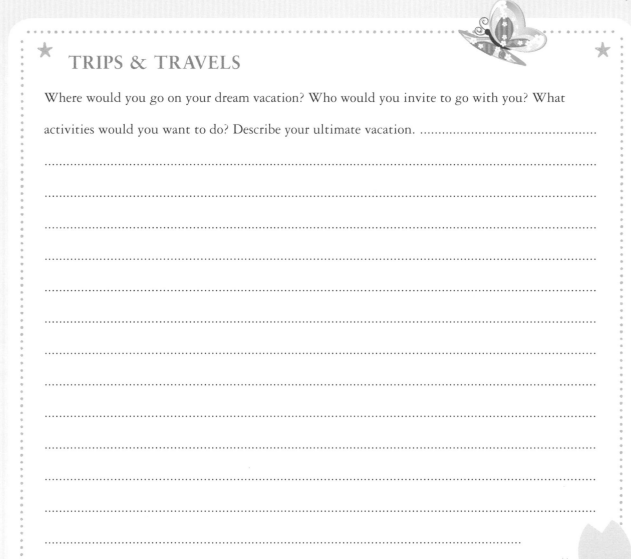

TRIPS & TRAVELS

Where would you go on your dream vacation? Who would you invite to go with you? What activities would you want to do? Describe your ultimate vacation. ....

....

....

....

....

....

....

....

....

....

....

....

....

....

TRIPS & TRAVELS

Write the first thing that comes to mind when you read these words …

museum: ....

hammock: ....

canyon: ....

tent: ....

yacht: ....

skiing: ....

lake: ....

waterfall: ....

countryside: ....

cabin: ....

shark: ....

seashell: ....

bicycle: ....

landmark: ....

luxury: ....

"The world is a book, and those who
do not travel read only a page." ~ St. Augustine

TRIPS & TRAVELS

If you were trapped on a desert island with only 5 possessions, what would they be, and why?

....

....

....

....

....

....

....

....

....

....

....

....

....

A LIFETIME OF FRIENDS

Who would you call your dearest friend? ....

What do you love about this person? ....

....

What qualities do you look for in friends? ....

....

Your favorite thing to do with friends: ....

....

What is one thing you have learned from your friendships? ....

....

A time when a friend was really there for you: ....

....

A close friend who has passed away: ....

What is the craziest thing you have ever done with a friend? ....

....

How you hope your friends would describe you: ....

....

"Let us be grateful to people who make us happy, they are the
charming gardeners who make our souls blossom." ~ Marcel Proust

A LIFETIME OF FRIENDS

Write a letter to a friend, either someone you are close with or someone you have grown apart from who you wish you could get in touch with. ....

....

....

....

....

....

....

....

....

....

....

....

....

....

FALLING IN LOVE

Who was your first crush? ....

How old were you? ....

Did he like you, too? ....

....

When was your first kiss? ....

....

At what age did your parents allow you to date? ....

Who was the first boy who took you on a date, and where did you go? ....

....

What was the best date spot in the town you grew up in? ....

....

Do you remember a terrible date you went on? ....

....

Did you ever think you were in love before meeting my father? ....

....

....

"Love doesn't make the world go round.
Love is what makes the ride worthwhile." ~ Franklin P. Jones

FALLING IN LOVE

Did you ever have a crush on a famous person as a young girl? Write about that funny crush and

how it developed. ....

....

....

....

....

....

....

....

....

....

....

....

....

....

....

FALLING IN LOVE

How and where did you meet my father? ....

....

What was your first thought when you met him? ....

....

....

Where did he take you on your first date? ....

....

When did you realize you wanted to see him again? ....

....

What did you like best about Dad? ....

....

What did your family think of him? ....

....

Were there any obstacles to your relationship? ....

....

How long was your courtship? ....

"Being in love shows a person who he should be."
~ Anton Chekov

FALLING IN LOVE

How did you know you were in love with my father? Describe any memories of your courtship.

....

....

....

....

....

....

....

....

....

....

....

....

....

....

FALLING IN LOVE

Describe the proposal: ....

....

Did he ask your parents' permission first? ....

What was your wedding date? ....

How old were you both? ....

Where did you get married? ....

Name a few special people who were there: ....

....

What did you wear? ....

Did you feel nervous about getting married? ....

....

What is your favorite memory of your wedding day? ....

....

....

Describe your wedding day in 3 words: ....

....

"If ever two were one, then surely we.
If ever man were loved by wife, then thee." ~ Anne Bradstreet

Place pictures
or mementos
from your
wedding day
here.

Your Wedding Day

NEWLYWEDS

Did you take a honeymoon? Where did you go? ....

....

Do you remember the first moment it hit you that you were married? ....

....

What was the best thing about being newlyweds? ....

....

What was the most unexpected or surprising thing about being married? ....

....

....

Did you learn anything new about him after you were married? ....

....

....

Did you find you had to change anything after marriage? ....

....

What was your toughest marital compromise? ....

....

*"To get the full value of joy you must
have someone to divide it with." ~ Mark Twain* ★

NEWLYWEDS

What do you believe are the keys to having a happy and successful marriage? Give your advice for

love and having a lifelong relationship. ....

....

....

....

....

....

....

....

....

....

....

....

....

....

★ NEWLYWEDS

Where did you live after the wedding? ....

....

Describe your first home as newlyweds: ....

....

What did you like about your first home? ....

....

What kind of home did you dream of having? ....

....

....

Do you still use any of your wedding gifts today? ....

What did you do for fun as a young married couple? ....

....

....

What other couples did you spend time with? ....

....

....

"Where we love is home, Home that our feet may leave, but not our hearts." ~ Oliver Wendell Holmes ★

Place a photo
of you as a
newlywed
couple here.

Newlyweds

BECOMING A MOM

When did you decide you wanted to have children? ....
....

Had you always wanted to be a mother or did the desire come later in life? ....
....

How many kids did you imagine yourself having? ....

How many boys and how many girls? ....

Describe your reaction to discovering you were pregnant with your first child: ....
....
....

How did Dad react? ....
....

What was your pregnancy with me like? Easy, difficult, exciting? ....
....
....

If I were to have been born the other sex, what would my name have been? ....
....

"Where there is love, there is life."
~ Gandhi

BECOMING A MOM

How did you settle on my name? What is its origin or meaning? What inspired it? What were

some other baby names you liked? ....

....

....

....

....

....

....

....

....

....

....

....

....

....

BECOMING A MOM

Was my birth difficult or a breeze? ....

....

Where was I born? ....

What time was I born? ....

Who was in the room during my birth? ....

What was your first reaction to holding me in your arms? ....

....

....

Describe the most surprising thing about being a mom: ....

....

What was the scariest thing? ....

....

The most wonderful thing? ....

....

What traits made you a good mother? ....

....

"When they placed you in my arms, you slipped into my heart."

~ Anonymous

Place a photo of me as an infant here.

Becoming a Mom

LOVING FAMILY

Describe me and each of my siblings in one word: ....

....

....

What advantages did we have as kids that you didn't have? ....

....

If you could change one thing about our childhood, what would it be? ....

....

....

What was your dream for me? ....

....

....

You always thought I would grow up to be: ....

Did I turn out as you expected? ....

What was our most memorable celebration as a family? ....

....

....

"We can do no great things; only small things with great love."
~ Mother Teresa

Place a photo
of me and my
siblings here.

The Kids

··

··

LOVING FAMILY

Describe a holiday tradition you enjoyed when we were kids: ....

....

What was your favorite thing about us as young kids? ....

....

....

Were we well-behaved children? ....

Who was the rebel in the family? ....

Who was a picky eater? ....

What did we do together as a family for fun? ....

....

What were our favorite board games? ....

....

Our favorite family TV shows? ....

....

Favorite family movies? ....

....

"Only a life lived for others is a life worthwhile."
~ Albert Einstein

LOVING FAMILY

What was your favorite family vacation we took? Why did you enjoy it so much? ....

....

....

....

....

....

....

....

....

....

....

....

....

....

....

LOVING FAMILY

What was your favorite age for us to be? ....

Describe a birthday party you remember having for me: ....

....

Do you remember a special dinner you used to cook the family? ....

....

Was having meals together important to you? ....

....

Did you and Dad ever have financial struggles? What did you do? ....

....

What was the toughest thing about running our household? ....

....

How did having a family change you? ....

....

....

What is the one thing you hoped to instill in us? ....

....

"If I had a flower for every time I thought of you,
I could walk in my garden forever." ~ Alfred Lord Tennyson

Place a photo of
our family here.

Family Memories

....

....

GROWING LIKE WEEDS

How did you feel when we were old enough to go off to school? ....

....

....

Do you remember a play or performance I was in? ....

....

Was there a particular outfit or article of clothing I refused to take off? ....

....

What was my favorite toy growing up? ....

Who was my favorite person to play with? ....

What was my favorite book? ....

What was my favorite game of make-believe? ....

....

What hobby did you hope I would take up, although I wasn't interested? ....

....

Did we move as our family grew? Where to? ....

....

"There is no friendship. no love, like that of a parent for the child."
~ Henry Ward Beecher

GROWING LIKE WEEDS

What was a major milestone in my life as a child or young person? How did I change? ....

....

....

....

....

....

....

....

....

....

....

....

....

....

GROWING LIKE WEEDS

Do you remember my first best friend? ....

Do you remember my first crush? ....

Describe a time you felt very protective of me: ....

....

When did I start to become truly independent? ....

....

Did you miss spending time with me as I grew up? ....

....

What hobbies did you find more time for as your children grew up? ....

....

....

Do you remember how it felt when I was ready to leave home? ....

....

Do you ever wish I was a kid again? ....

....

....

"The child must know that he is a miracle, that since the
beginning of the world there hasn't been, and until the end of the
world there will not be, another child like him." ~ Pablo Casals

Place a reminder
of a time when
you were most
proud
of me here.

A Proud Moment

....

....

★ FAVORITES

Quote: ....

....

Color: ....

Number: ....

Meal: ....

Snack: ....

Dessert: ....

Flavor of ice cream: ....

Fruit: ....

Vegetable: ....

Holiday: ....

Way to relax: ....

Gift you've been given: ....

Actor: ....

Actress: ....

Day of the week: ....

"And these are a few of my favorite things ..."
~ The Sound of Music ★

FAVORITES

Animal: ....

Clothing designer: ....

City: ....

State: ....

National park: ....

Cereal: ....

Flower: ....

Beauty product: ....

Pizza topping: ....

Board game: ....

Car: ....

Hobby: ....

Magazine: ....

Cocktail: ....

Snack: ....

Book: ....

Song: ....

★ FAVORITES

Month: ....

Season: ....

Website: ....

Store: ....

Restaurant: ....

Sundae topping: ....

Fictional character: ....

Musical group: ....

Country: ....

Guilty pleasure: ....

Sport: ....

Athlete: ....

TV show: ....

Movie: ....

Thing to do on a rainy day: ....

Scent: ....

*"Enjoy the little things, for one day you may
look back and realize they were the big things."* ~ Robert Brault ★

Place a
favorite piece of
memorabilia here.

Favorites

★ HAVE YOU EVER ...

Write down "yes" or "no" for the following questions:

Eaten a bug: ....

Been in a car accident: ....

Acted in a play: ....

Flown in a helicopter: ....

Sung karaoke: ....

Eaten rabbit: ....

Been to Paris: ....

Won a sweepstakes: ....

Had an article written about you: ....

Been arrested: ....

Published a book: ....

Shot a gun: ....

Caught a butterfly: ....

Seen a ghost: ....

Skinny-dipped: ....

Baked a pie: ....

Jumped rope: ....

Been a vegetarian: ....

Climbed a mountain: ....

Eaten frog's legs: ....

Been a bridesmaid: ....

Had a pet bird: ....

Had your heart broken: ....

Gone waterskiing: ....

Done yoga: ....

Regretted saying "I love you": ....

Held a snake: ....

Ridden a motorcycle: ....

Fainted: ....

Swam in the ocean: ....

"One way to get the most out of life is
to look upon it as an adventure." ~ William Feather ★

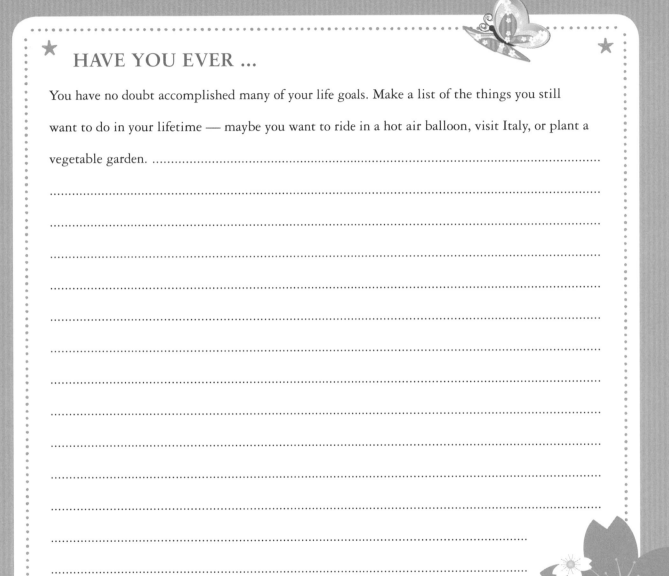

HAVE YOU EVER ...

You have no doubt accomplished many of your life goals. Make a list of the things you still want to do in your lifetime — maybe you want to ride in a hot air balloon, visit Italy, or plant a vegetable garden. ....

....

....

....

....

....

....

....

....

....

....

....

....

★ HAVE YOU EVER ...

Write down "yes" or "no" for the following questions:

Been scuba diving: ....

Fixed a flat tire: ....

Run a marathon: ....

Ridden a horse: ....

Shoplifted: ....

Received a dozen roses: ....

Won a spelling bee: ....

Been in a bowling league: ....

Done a backflip: ....

Had a surprise birthday party: ....

Seen a whale: ....

Paddled a canoe: ....

Drank tequila: ....

Visited Japan: ....

Ate sushi: ....

Gambled: ....

Ridden in an ambulance: ....

Gotten a terrible haircut: ....

Broken a bone: ....

Received a love letter: ....

Gone to a baseball game: ....

Been superstitious: ....

Sent a text message: ....

Eaten anchovies: ....

Found a $20 bill: ....

Talked to God: ....

Fell down a flight of stairs: ....

Been on a blind date: ....

Knit a scarf: ....

Gone camping: ....

"Freedom lies in being bold." ~ Robert Frost ★

Place a photo or cut-out that represents something crazy you have done here.

A Wonderful Adventure

....

....

★ FANTASY!

Did you ever dream of being a star? ....

....

What film would you have loved to have been in? ....

Have you ever met someone famous? ....

....

What did you think of that person afterward? ....

....

Something you wish you'd invented: ....

If you could fly, where would you go? ....

....

If you won $1 million, what is the first thing you would do? ....

....

If you could be a man for one day, what would you do? ....

....

If you could make one food calorie-free, what would you choose? ....

....

"Life is magic, the way nature works seems to be quite magical."
~ Jonas Salk ★

FANTASY!

A genie appears and grants you three wishes. What do you ask for? ....

....

....

....

....

....

....

....

....

....

....

....

....

....

....

....

....

★ FANTASY!

What would you do if money were no object? ....

....

....

Which celebrity would play you in a movie about your life? ....

What would the movie be called? ....

Would it be a comedy, drama, Western? ....

....

If you could choose, what animal would you be? ....

What flower would you be? ....

If you could have one superpower, what would it be? ....

....

If you could travel back or forward in time, what era would you visit? ....

....

....

If you were invisible, what would you do? ....

....

"I like nonsense, it wakes up the brain cells.
Fantasy is a necessary ingredient in living." ~ Dr. Seuss ★

FANTASY!

You are hosting a dinner party — what three people, dead or alive, would you invite, and why?

⭐ WORDS OF WISDOM

What person in your life has given you the best advice over the years, and what was it? ....

....

....

Who has had the biggest influence? ....

....

Who has been most supportive of you? ....

Who do you admire the most, and why? ....

....

What is your best advice on love? ....

....

Best advice on money? ....

....

Best advice on career? ....

....

What is the one thing in your life you would change? ....

....

"People grow through experience if they meet life honestly and
courageously. This is how character is built." ~ Eleanor Roosevelt ★

WORDS OF WISDOM

What do you believe are the keys to being happy and loving life? ....

....

....

....

....

....

....

....

....

....

....

....

....

....

....

★ WORDS OF WISDOM

What fears or obstacles have you had to overcome to be happy? ....

....

....

What accomplishment are you are the most proud of? ....

....

....

Is there anything in your past that you now view as a blessing in disguise? ....

....

....

What are you thankful that we had that you didn't growing up? ....

....

What is one aspect of modern technology that you are grateful for? ....

....

At what age did you feel like you really came into your own? ....

....

....

"Life is a sum of all your choices."
~ Albert Camus ★

Place a photo
that represents
your biggest
blessings here.

Life's Blessings

HOPES FOR THE FUTURE

Describe a few of your goals for the future: ....

....

....

....

What is the next vacation you plan to take? ....

....

Name one hobby you would like to take up in the next year: ....

....

Name one bad habit you would like to break: ....

....

What is the next thing you will save up for? ....

Is there something you've been putting off that you can finish? ....

....

What is a tradition you would like to keep in coming years? ....

....

....

"He who is not everyday conquering some fear
has not learned the secret of life." ~ Ralph Waldo Emerson

HOPES FOR THE FUTURE

Write a letter to the greatest loves in your life. What do you want to tell them? What can you

thank them for? ....

....

....

....

....

....

....

....

....

....

....

....

....

HOPES FOR THE FUTURE

What is your greatest hope for your children? ....

....

What is one thing you would like to learn? ....

....

One person you would like to spend more time with: ....

In 10 years, where do you see yourself? ....

....

What do you like the most (or look forward to the most) about having grandchildren? ....

....

....

What fortune would you like to find in your fortune cookie? ....

....

....

How would you like to be remembered? ....

....

....

*"The consciousness of loving and being loved brings a warmth
and richness to life that nothing else brings."* ~ Oscar Wilde